Untold Secrets from My Past

Alysha Drummond

Presentation by *BookLeaf Publishing*

Web: www.bookleafpub.com

E-mail: info@bookleafpub.com

ISBN: 9789357610957

First edition 2022

DEDICATION

To those suffering within searching for peace. We all have our battles we must eventually conquer. There is no time limit on healing. Though you must heal from within in order to move forward.

ACKNOWLEDGEMENT

A Thank You to my family and fellow supporters.

PREFACE

In, "Untold Secrets from My Past", we experience depression, anxiety, personality changes and how trauma can impact a person's life with time. We base the story around Honesty and her traumatic childhood. Some content may be triggering to readers. We follow along with her as we read about her depression, confusion, feelings of hopelessness, love and the future she looks forward to having when she decides to let go of her hurt. Forgiving herself seems to be the first task but choosing to move forward; will ultimately be her greatest challenge.

The Day I Lost my Sanity

To be sane is offensive to me...we are all slightly
insane in some ways.
I believe that time is made for the immortal.
Well, since I am a mortal being—
I suppose time is not meant for me.
So here we are—Timeless.
I often feel as if I am a prisoner to my own
mind.
I have held myself captive long enough.
I decided that freeing my mind will bring me a
sense of clarity.
Clarity reveals an even deeper pain,
One that I had not prepared for.
So, I fall.
Sinking into my bucket full of issues.
I allow them to consume me.
I have no time left—
Time appears too only be endless to the
fortunate ones...
I seem to be one of the unfortunate ones in this
situation.
I decided that instead of trying to become one
with myself and my thoughts,
I would instead detach completely from my
body.
Mentally insane.

I watch as my soul desperately departs away
from me.
Attempting to grab a hold of her—
I fail.
Seems my time is up.
Soulless…
Emptily I travel this world attempting to find the
piece of me that was taken.
Finding purpose once again will be my next
task.

Silent Screams

3

I am crying for help, but no one seems to hear
me.
No one cares to listen.
How do you scream aloud when your mouth is
stitched shut?
How do you cry when you are blind folded?
How do you escape when you are being held
down.
Alone...
Trapped.
Angry for no apparent reason at all...
Though in all actuality—
There is a reason.
I just haven't figured it out yet.

Dissociative Mind

That dissociative state.
That one where your mind leads you.
Unable to distinguish if it was your mind or
body speaking for you—
Or if you are just lost and speaking for yourself.
It's a constant circle..
Like a tornado that refuses to end until it has
done its damage.
Then again…
How much damage can the human mind do.
Pacing back and forth mumbling, "What do you
expect me to do?"
As I sit here I think,
Where is this coming from.
I guess it was all too much to keep bottled in.
When those secrets start to invade your soul—
When you discover someone other than
yourself—
You begin to look for any possible way out.
When the only way out is for you to recognize
yourself.
This dissociative mind is something new to me.
Apparently its wants were needed desperately.
I find myself lost and unsure.
I am forced to deal with the dissociation...

Trying to fight it as if I had the upper hand..
Unfortunately, I don't have much will power.
My heart is cold and guarded.
Pain, torture, and hurt..
Constantly put upon me...
Guards put up around me...
Just to stop intruders from invading.
Dissociative states protect me...
Blocking the real me...
Disguising the real me...
This dissociative state won't live with me.
For it is not a fear of me..
It will live in the past.

Fool's Paradise

I was once told I was too soft–
Too gullible–
Too accepting–
Too nice.
So when you hear enough of what you ARE you
begin to reanalyze.
Am I too soft?
Gullible?
Nice? Accepting?
You then begin to create an image that is suitable
for others.
One that shows you stand your ground.
One that shows you care only about what is
beneficial to you.
An image built to cover up the person you really
are.
Being that your true self had to be hidden for so
long…
You are now left with crumbles of your past
life…
Welcome to the one you created.
Fool's Paradise.

Dreaming

Startled.
I wake up.
It grazes my thigh with passion..
Your fingertips.
I am scared but I know better then to say
anything.
Why should I?
Even though I am the one being violated.
Even though I am the one that wanted help— I
knew I couldn't get it.
Who would have believed me?
They may think I'm like all the other false
accusers.
So again who would believe me….
I barely believe it happened myself.

Just One More

To feel free, she must first be relieved of all her pain.
Her worries-- they seem to follow her.
She decides one pill won't hurt.
One pill.
A pill that has the luxury of unleashing her unforgiving moments.
She can live once more.
She can hold on just a few more hours.
She can be in her own world.
She is free from her mind…
That is until her loneliness begins to seep through.

Antidote

9

She struggles mentally to find herself.
She's been taught "coping strategies" and she's been told how to cope.
She's been shown how to "handle stressful situations".; though she has found that It doesn't help.
The only way she seems to cope is by becoming one with her current choice of beverage.
The only thing she seems to "handle"; is the bottle of vodka she is pouring in her cup.
This is the only way she has learned to cope.
Nothing else seems to be beneficial to her life.
Maybe she hasn't given any of it any effort.
She drinks until her vision is blurry and this gives her a sense of peace.
Alcohol seems to be her only antidote.
Popping pills seems to be her only relief— for the time being.
She's learned how to handle these things in her own way.
Her antidote is slowly driving her closer to her death bed...
But it works for her.

A Brief Statement

I've tried the therapy shit.
It just didn't work for me.
I sat alone crying for hours as we made
meaningful steps together—
My therapist and I.
We agreed that I would face him.
We agreed that it would be better for me to
confront him.
I couldn't do it.
How do you remind someone of the trauma you
once lived.
How do you remind them of their decisions?
So fuck it.
Fuck therapy too.
It's easier to forget.

Darkness

I feel the darkness over me.
Hovering over me as if I am it's next victim.
I spend every waking moment trying to shake
it's hold off of me–
I am failing miserably at surviving.
I feel its anxiousness.
Waiting on me to fall victim to its games…
Eager for me to say, "Take Me."
I can't.
I can't allow it to control me—
Consume me and create this monster I have been
fighting against for years.
It smells me.
It caresses me with sweet lullabies as I doze off
to sleep.
It preys on me.
Staring as my eyes are closed…
Watching me as I dream.
Listening to me plea for help.
Laughing as it watches me go mentally insane.
The darkness.
Wondering how is it that I can mange to hold it
together.
Why is it that I won't allow it to consume me.

Why won't I allow my light to become
darkness?
Evil creeps in the night.
Darkness leads the way.
Though they are eager to both reach my light…
The longer it creeps…
The further away I seem.
The darkness..
Ready to take over me…
My light shines brighter.
I am much stronger than they expected.
It was easy to underestimate my strength since
they preyed on my motionless body.
Eager to have what it can't.
The darkness continues to creep…
Searching for its next victim.

My Diary: Truth Be Told?

Page 3 of 30 from My Diary...

Honesty writes:

Fuck this life. Being molded as a child…Can we talk about that? I mean is the topic too sensitive? Or is it the fact that we undermine what is actually going on. In homes and around us. Or would this be a perfect time to say, "What goes on in this house stays in this house." I have lived life in fear. I wouldn't say that in a literal way simply because of the life I was forced to create for myself. FORCED. Why? The odds were against me the moment he decided to touch me. Who was ever going to believe me? A young girl that didn't ask for any of this but yet I received it all. I ask myself at times why me? Why was I chosen to silently suffer? There is so much that I wish I could say but I just can't. I find it difficult to explain it in words. When I started therapy she said that it would be best to confront my fears and my abuser and forgive them. While that sounds good…I can't. In this life I created an image of them that is noble. An image that can be easily digested. In all honesty they are the same as they were years ago…they just hide it well.

I wonder if they were touched on as a child? Those habits stem from somewhere right? I think I spent so much time beating and blaming myself for what happened, that I forgot to acknowledge that it wasn't my fault. I didn't ask for any of it. While it may seem that I am rambling I am sure most of this will make sense in the end. I had to create a false reality in order to mentally digest my own. It became me…I forgot all about who I used to be. I left that little girl all alone…abandoned; in her room crying. I'm sorry Honesty. I should have came forward.

My Suicide Note

This...
It's going to be hard to understand.
But this is..
My suicide note.
Because I feel like I don't have anything to live
for—
A reason to move on...
No one to be there for.
See I've molded myself into this...
"Person".
Who tends to look over their feelings for others.
I'm trying to wrap my mind around how I could
even feel like I can't be here anymore...
But, unfortunately...
That's what it is.
Where I stand now with these words—
Is a difficult place.
Because no one is trying to understand.
It hurts me to tell you that this is how I feel but
to be real...
It's just..
No way to fight it.
So this—
Is my suicide note.
Just in case you were wondering.

If I'm to that point...
I'm there now.

I feel like everyone around me that I've been
befriending,
Caring about..
And loving too.
They've failed me in the end.
I've tried to be a good friend.
I have some good friends but then...
Those same "friends"...
Don't look at it that way.
So this is my suicide note.
Don't say Goodbye now.
Because when I needed you there...
You weren't around.
You can't save me.
I can't save me.
Only God knows where I'll end up...
And it's sad to say it has to be this way.
But unfortunately...
I've given up.

A Letter to My Depression

To my depression,
You CAN'T control me...
No matter how much you think you can.
Letting you win shows I failed,
I can't allow you to take control of my life
anymore.
It's non-negotiable.
I'm trying to take back every piece that I've left,
That I've lost,
I'm trying to pick up those pieces to the puzzle
that I dropped years ago..
I find myself lost so often that sometimes I don't
even know which way to go
So this is my letter to you.
As I can't keep going on like this anymore,
Sometimes I wake up—
Sometimes I just randomly cry not knowing
why, but I know why...
Because I feel like I'm not fulfilling my purpose.
But I am…it's just that damn depression.
You got a way of showing your ass,
You got a way of "showing up and showing out"
and not leaving until you have ruined everything
possible.

Then we are left to decide whether being here is
worth it...
And it is.
This is my letter to you,
My Depression.
I have dealt with you way too long—
Yes you will always be a part of me but I'm
going to leave you with this letter.
I'm going to drop it off in your mailbox so you
know not to fuck with me.
I'm going to leave it for you so you don't have to
bother me.
This is me warning you— you no longer have
control of me.
I let you win your battle in your lane—
As I'm winning those in mine.
I survived...
You cant control me.
You cant hold me,
Anything you do is to persuade me into loving
you...
Not myself…
So this is my letter to you.
To my Depression,
I've learned my lesson.

A Tear Never Last

I cried today...
Not for sympathy...
Not for looks...
You know…those same looks people give when
they feel you want attention...
That same looks they give you when they fail to
understand what you are going through?
Well, I understand.
I understand that today I cried for me.
Not because I feel alone...
But because I fear to be alone.
Not because of those who said they cared...
Then walked off without a warning.
Not because I feel anger...
And lash out with no warning.
Not because, "Life gets tough"...
It is because people think they know you based
off what they know of you...
Because they know of your tendencies.
Those pitiful ways they portrayed me.
I cried for me.
I cried because sometimes anxiety is hard to
handle...
Although no one sees your constant battles.
It's those times you don't see..

Those times where everything appears to me as
a blur.
Those times when you are forced to hold your
head up,
Even when you want to let it down.
Those times where you want to scream—
When you are alone.
Those times when you realize you are truly lost.
You spend so much time thinking that you are
the problem...
You create a hole for yourself...
One you must find your way out of.
I cried for the crazy girl everyone speaks of...
In that moment, I decided I wanted to live
instead of die.
I came to the realization that I can't do it on my
own...
I cried for the girl that once lived inside of me...
I cried for me.

Late Night Hallucinations

A travel back to reality.
A reality I once knew as my own, replaced; in order to keep me safe.
I have difficulty distinguishing the difference between my reality and the one which I've created...
A way to escape.
This can't be my only escape?
Why me?
What did I do to deserve a treatment of this sort?
I find myself forgetting every good memory.
I find myself forgetting years of sweet innocence.
I find myself forgetting me.
I was forced to go there, to my escape.
When the mind has no choice—it recedes within itself.
So that it did.
Forced to eliminate all experiences—
Leaving me there to create new ones.
With these new thoughts,
I knew that it was impossible to speak on what I knew.

How can you speak on something you know,
when everything you once knew has begun to
disintegrate?
For years, I denigrated along with it.
Sometimes when I speak on it—
I can still feel the hands.
I can still feel the breathing on my neck.
I can feel my body shifting and moving.
Not on my account but yours.
I still feel your parts pushed against mine.
I still feel my clothes— leaving me.
Piece by piece.
I feel my mind drifting away from this...
I can still feel the tears on my cheek from the
day you almost took it too far.
I still feel you in some part of my unconscious
mind.
Late night hallucinations have forced me to
believe that this is only a reality that lives in one
area of my mind.
An area that I lost.
A section that I mentally carved out and threw in
the trash.
Its debris seems to slowly find its way back in
my life.
Forcing me to remember what it was like.
What it was like to be helpless because I was
afraid to say anything,
Afraid that it would be considered a lie.

Fighting between reality and my alternate
reality.
Debating on if it is worth returning back to what
it was before.
I'm better in an alternate life.
Late night hallucinations haunt me.
While one piece was lost—
A new hallucination was found.

My Diary: Letting Go…

Honesty writes:

In order to completely let go and find peace with the situation I had to find a way to release. I have dealt with this pain for so long. Sometimes I even feel like the events that happened never happened. I have been succumbed by this reality I created for myself that I feel like what happened didn't. I have made myself believe it. Well…it did happen. It happened to me and I forgave them because I knew that no one would believe me. So here goes….I wasn't raped but I was molested. I was touched on by someone who looked at me as if I were an adult. It's sad that I felt I couldn't tell anyone. I had to live like this. I had to ask countless question. Why? This was the main question I asked. Why me and why did I stay quiet? I reminisce now on how bubbly I was back then. How happy I was. Now I am just trying to figure out how to let go and live life. Shit happens. It really does. Instead of inflicting the same pain on them as they did me;

I decided to forgive them. God will deal with them.
I decided to let it go. Along with every possible image I created of them. To me...they have become a distant memory. Only fragments of their face remain. I think this is called healing?

A Letter to Me

We have come to a very difficult road…
We have crossed it before.
Though it feels this time it's impossible.
It's okay to be disappointed,
It's ok to be ashamed,
It's okay to say— "I'm not okay."
I sit here,
As I let my lost mind wonder and I gaze off.
It's okay—
Not to be okay.
I must admit it to myself.
That I'm not okay and I'm lost.
This is not the first time I have felt this way..
I feel lost very often.
But now?
It's hard to find my way back.
It's difficult for me to understand why I continue
to fail…
Why I continue to love…
And no love is returned.
Maybe I'm missing the signs…
Maybe I'm looking for the wrong "him"
Because "he" was shown too early…
"He" is the epitome of my pain…

"He" showed me what it felt like to be
helpless…
"He" molded me…at an age I could not
understand…
He is still within me.
Because of him, this endless cycle of bad events
continue to occur…
And I let it.
Believing I was looking for him all long…
When I couldn't even find myself…
I am sorry.
Somewhere along the way I lost my grip— of
you.
I am sorry if I let you down and disappointed
you…
I wasn't mature enough back then.
I am sorry I wasn't brave enough to set us free…
Though when we look at it, how free are we?
When the odds are against us…
When we are the blame for everything…
When we are liars..
I am sorry you couldn't be yourself around me.
I am sorry for the little girl that cries tears of
pain…
Wondering why love never chose her..
I am sorry you are so unhappy.
I am sorry you are alone.
Self…
I want you to see your potential…

I want you to see just how valuable you are.
I want you to see that you are love.
I am sorry I couldn't guide you the way you
needed to be…
But I am here now.

Peace and Serenity

I've found myself at peace for once,
Alone and in my home.
I prefer things to be this way.
I have lived a split life for so long…
It seems that I have forgotten how to interact
with others.
So here I am.
Since a temper won't settle any of my battles…
I sit calmly...
In sync with my troubling thoughts.
I cry...
Allowing myself to feel.
Allowing myself to be in this moment.
I slowly let go of this pain I have felt for so
long…
Through my tears— I remain sane.
My serenity counts on it.
I walk amongst those who prey on that
loneliness I feel quite often.
I search for my peace in the midst of this tragedy
I call life…
My peace must be kept at all times.

In Time

Though I have been at my lowest
Now in this moment I feel a sense of clarity
Id like to think that I am healing...
Though I could never be too sure.
I have failed time after time trying to get this
right.
How to cope,
How to live,
How to love someone even though I don't love
myself.
I understand that it takes time to get here and
without time…
We fail to exist.

Cloudy

I look out…
As I am mesmerized by this beautiful sky,
I see HOPE.
This beautiful creation.
One that can be so gloomy and grey.
One that can cause such an ugly storm,
And yet, bring such a breathtaking sight.
I look towards the sky.
I stare at the clouds as they slowly move.
I create these images in my head.
Images of what I see— what I feel.
I can say, these are the moments I am grateful
for.
This view, it is like many others– beautiful.
The clouds— they calm you.
In the distance,
I see one in particular that catches my eye.
I wish it were closer.
I wish I could touch it.
I wish…
I wish only to travel these beautiful blues skies
like the clouds.
Gracefully and free.